MY FIRST LOOK AT PLANETS

URANUS LOOKS DARK WHEN IT IS NOT IN SUNLIGHT

Uranus

TERESA WIMMER

CREATIVE EDUCATION

Published by Creative Education

P.O. Box 227, Mankato, Minnesota 56002

Creative Education is an imprint of The Creative Company

Designed by Rita Marshall

Photographs by Library of Congress, Photo Researchers (Julian Baum / Science Photo

Library, NASA / Science Photo Library, NASA / Science Source, John Sanford / Science

Photo Library), Tom Stack & Associates (NASA / JPL, Therisa Stack / TSADO / NASA,

TSADO / NASA)

Printed in the United States of America

Library of Congress Cataloging-in-Publication Data

Wimmer, Teresa, 1975- Uranus / by Teresa Wimmer.

p. cm. — (My first look at planets)

Includes index.

ISBN-13: 978-1-58341-523-8

1. Uranus (Planet)—Juvenile literature. I. Title.

QB681.W56 2007   523.47—dc22   2006018708

First edition 9 8 7 6 5 4 3 2 1

Uranus

Far Out

At night, people can see a tiny dot in the dark sky. That dot is really a big **planet** called Uranus. It is far away from Earth. That makes it look very small. But Uranus is a lot bigger than Earth.

Uranus is part of the **solar system**. Besides Uranus, there are seven other planets. All of the planets move in an **orbit** around the sun. Uranus is the seventh planet from the sun.

FROM URANUS, THE SUN LOOKS VERY SMALL

Uranus is far away from the sun. That means it has a long way to go around the sun. It takes 84 Earth years for Uranus to go around the sun once! It takes Earth only one year.

ICY COLD

Up close, Uranus looks like a blue ball. It is made of **gas** and slushy liquid. The gas makes Uranus look pretty.

Half of Uranus has 42 years of daytime. The other half has 42 years of nighttime. Then they switch.

The gas on Uranus would hurt people. People could not breathe the gas and live. That is why no people live on Uranus. There are no animals or plants there, either.

Uranus does not get much of the sun's heat. That means it is a very cold planet. Clouds cover most of Uranus. Sometimes Uranus has big storms, too. The storms have strong, cold winds. They happen everywhere on the planet.

Some people think Uranus

might have a lot of

water under its clouds.

Rings and Moons

One thing makes Uranus different from all of the other planets. Uranus looks tipped over in the sky. Most planets spin like tops in the sky. But Uranus looks like it is rolling on its side.

Eleven rings circle Uranus. The rings are made of tiny rocks. That makes them look very dark. The rings are very thin, too. Sometimes it looks like Uranus is rolling through hoops in the sky!

People think a big rock crashed

into Uranus a long time ago.

It knocked Uranus over.

Uranus has at least 27 moons. The moons move in an orbit around Uranus. One of the biggest moons is named Miranda. It is made of rock and ice.

ARTISTS IMAGINE HOW URANUS LOOKS FROM ICY MIRANDA

There is still a lot that people do not know about Uranus. They send **probes** there. The probes have special cameras. The cameras take pictures that show more of Uranus.

Uranus is a long way from Earth. It takes many years for a probe to get there. One probe has flown by Uranus a few times. Each time, it found more moons and rings.

Some of Uranus's moons
are very small. They
move in its rings.

URANUS (THIRD FROM LEFT) IS THE THIRD-BIGGEST PLANET

Someday, more probes will be sent to Uranus. The probes might be able to get very close to the planet. They might find even more moons and rings around Uranus!

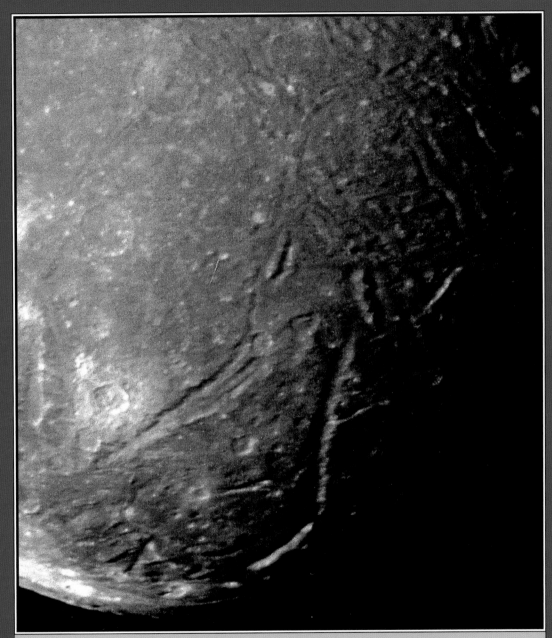

A PROBE TOOK PICTURES OF URANUS'S MOON ARIEL

Hands-on: Make a Planet Uranus

Uranus is a pretty planet. You can make your very own planet Uranus!

What You Need

A big Styrofoam ball

A piece of yarn about eight inches (20 cm) long

A yellow marker

A blue marker

One gray, one brown, and two white pipe cleaners

Glue

What You Do

1. Color the Styrofoam ball blue.
2. Glue one white pipe cleaner around the middle of the ball. Glue the gray and brown pipe cleaners on top of the white one. Glue the other white pipe cleaner on top of them.
3. Glue one end of the yarn to the top of the ball.
4. Now you have your own planet Uranus!

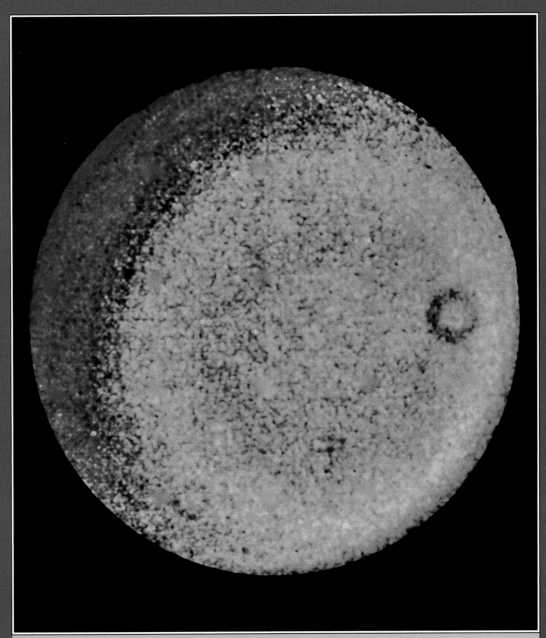

URANUS IS AN INTERESTING PLANET TO STUDY

Index

Words to Know

gas—a kind of air; some gases are harmful to breathe

orbit—the path a planet takes around the sun or a moon takes around a planet

planet—a round object that moves around the sun

probes—special machines that fly around or land on a planet or a moon

solar system—the sun, the planets, and their moons

Read More

Rudy, Lisa Jo. *Planets!* New York: HarperCollins, 2005.

Taylor-Butler, Christine. *Uranus.* New York: Scholastic, 2005.

Vogt, Gregory. *Solar System.* New York: Scholastic, 2001.

Explore the Web

Enchanted Learning: Uranus http://www.zoomschool.com/subjects/astronomy/planets/uranus

Funschool: Space http://funschool.kaboose.com/globe-rider/space/index.html?trnstl=1

StarChild: The Planet Uranus http://starchild.gsfc.nasa.gov/docs/StarChild/solar_system_level1/uranus.html